THE
ARMOR OF GOD

HEAVEN'S DESIGN FOR VICTORY
A SCRIPTURAL AND SPIRITUAL BLUEPRINT
FROM THE WRITINGS OF DAMIANO B. CENTOLA

DAMIANO B. CENTOLA

EXPLORA BOOKS
700 – 838 West Hastings St. Vancouver
BC V6C 0A6
www.explorabooks.com
Phone: (604) 330 6795

Because of the dynamic nature of the Internet, any web addresses or links contained in this book may have changed since publication and may no longer be valid. The views expressed in this work are solely those of the author and do not necessarily reflect the views of the publisher, and the publisher hereby disclaims any responsibility for them.

Bible verses are quoted from the King James Version (KJV), which is public domain, the English Standard Version (ESV), and the New King James Version (NKJV).

ISBN: 978-1-997587-97-2 (*Paperback*)
978-1-83430-016-0 (*Hardback*)
978-1-83430-017-7 (*eBook*)

THE
ARMOR OF GOD

DEDICATION

To Feebe,

Whose prayers gird me daily with unseen strength, whose love is my shelter in every battle, and whose faith walks beside mine—step for step.

To the Remnant,

Who still stand when the world bows, who still believe when the fire burns hot, and who wear Heaven's armor not for show—but for war.

And to the Commander of the Host, Jesus Christ—my covering, my courage, and my eternal Victor.

TABLE OF CONTENTS

ACKNOWLEDGEMENTS

To the One who teaches my hands to war and my fingers to fight—

Yeshua, the Captain of my salvation—this work belongs to You.

To Feebe, my beloved, who lives this battle beside me in prayer, patience, and fierce love. Your courage wraps around my weakness like armor forged in heaven.

To my spiritual family—watchmen, intercessors, truth-bearers, and warriors of light—thank you for standing in the gap, for contending in silence, and for never laying down your sword.

To Paula Garcia and the entire team at Explora Books, thank you for your relentless belief in the power of words and the power of God behind them.

To every scholar, pastor, prophet, and friend who has poured wisdom into my journey—your deposits have become weapons in this book.

And to every reader—may you not just read these pages, but stand because of them.

PREFACE

There comes a moment in every believer's life when passivity must give way to purpose, when casual Christianity is no longer an option, and when heaven's call to stand becomes louder than earth's pressure to retreat. I have lived that moment. And if you're holding this book, I believe you have too.

This is not a book about ancient armor; it's about divine design. It's not a metaphor—it's a mandate. The Apostle Paul was not writing poetry when he penned the words of Ephesians 6; he was issuing marching orders from a Roman prison cell to a generation of spiritual warriors. Each piece of the armor he describes is not ornamental—it is essential. Heaven does not dress its soldiers in suggestion, but in substance. This is the uniform of the remnant. This is the attire of those who carry the weight of intercession, the authority of truth, and the fire of the living God.

Over the years, I have poured my soul into writing about the prophetic voice (The Voice in the Wilderness), the war on conscience (Selective Outrage), the holy remnant (Bloodline), and the mysteries of Christ in body and spirit (Mystery of Mysteries, Son of Man, The Bread of Life). But never before have I been drawn to distill it all into one unified design—the armor that holds it all together. In these pages, I trace each weapon and covering with theological clarity and prophetic urgency, anchoring every insight in Scripture and cross-referencing it with the journey God has had me walk.

You will see familiar themes here—truth, righteousness, faith, salvation, prayer—not as abstract doctrines, but as divine materials forged in fire for the battlefield. These are not ideas to be admired; they are realities to be worn.

This book is for the watchman on the wall, the intercessor in the hidden place, the pastor worn from battle, the young believer hungry to stand firm, and the mother weeping for her children in the midnight hour. It is for anyone who knows deep down: we are not in a season of peace, but of preparation.

The war is not coming—it has already begun. But so has the revealing of the sons and daughters of God. And their armor, beloved, is ready.

—Damiano B. Centola

INTRODUCTION
The Invisible War and the Divine Wardrobe

We do not live in neutral times. The air is thick with deception, and the battle lines are not drawn with ink, but with blood, truth, and eternity. What the Apostle Paul wrote nearly two thousand years ago remains burning with present relevance:

> *"For we wrestle not against flesh and blood, but against*
> *principalities, against powers, against the rulers of*
> *the darkness of this world, against spiritual*
> *wickedness in high places."*
> *—Ephesians 6:12 (KJV)*

This war is not metaphorical. It is invisible—but intensely real. And in it, every believer must be dressed for divine engagement. This is not a call to aggression but to awareness, not to militancy but to maturity. The armor of God is not about conquest—it is about standing.

To stand, when the world collapses.

To stand, when your mind is assaulted.

To stand, when temptation screams louder than conscience.

To stand, when lies are praised and truth is punished.

To stand, not in your own strength, but in the full armor of God.

This book explores the ancient, unbreakable design of that armor—crafted not by Roman blacksmiths, but by the mind of God. Each piece is theological and practical, symbolic yet solid. The belt of truth, the breastplate of righteousness, the shoes of the gospel of peace, the shield of faith, the helmet of salvation, the sword of the Spirit—and the one piece often overlooked: prayer in the Spirit.

But more than that, this book brings together the threads from my prior works—on truth, conscience, righteousness, identity, prayer, and the prophetic voice—and weaves them into one garment: the armor that heaven gives to its warriors.

Each chapter will examine one element of the armor through three lenses:

1. Biblical Foundation – Where it originates and what Scripture reveals.

2. Practical Equipping – How to wear it daily.

3. Prophetic Significance – Why it matters right now in this generation.

We are not here to survive—we are here to stand and overcome. The armor is not a costume—it is covenant. It is heaven's seal upon the life of the redeemed. And it is time to put it on.

Let us begin where Paul began—not with the sword, but with the belt. Truth first. Always.

—Damiano B. Centola

Chapter I
The Belt of Truth —
Girded for Integrity

"Stand therefore, having your loins girt about with
truth..."
—Ephesians 6:14 (KJV)

The First Piece of the Armor

When Paul describes the armor of God, he does not begin with a shield or
sword. He does not rush to helmets or breastplates. He begins with the
belt—a detail that would seem minor in any ordinary battle formation, but
not in heaven's economy. In the Kingdom of God, truth holds everything
together.

The belt of truth is not merely decorative. It is central. It girds the loins—
symbolically the seat of strength, reproduction, and identity. It secures all
other armor and allows free, focused movement in battle. Without the belt,
the warrior is exposed. The armor shifts. The posture weakens. And the
enemy finds a gap.

So Paul says, "Stand therefore..." Not kneel, not retreat. Stand. And to
stand, one must be girded—tightened and fastened—with truth.

Girding for Battle: A Call to Integrity

In Selective Outrage, I wrote that the erosion of truth is the erosion of civilization. When we selectively apply truth—truth for one group and not another, truth for convenience and not for conviction—we are not girded. We are unbuckled, vulnerable, and compromised. Truth is not optional. It is oxygen.

In The Voice in the Wilderness, I described the prophets as those who carried truth like fire in their bones. They did not bend. They did not twist. They did not appease. They declared the unbending truth of God, even when it cost them their reputation, safety, or life.

That's what it means to be girded: truth that tightens you into integrity. It is truth that keeps your inner life and outer life from splitting apart.

This is more than doctrinal truth. It is moral truth. Personal truth. It is the alignment of your private world with your public stance. It is not simply what you say. It is who you are when no one sees. The belt of truth is not just for defense—it is for dignity.

TRUTH

DC

Truth Is Not a Weapon; It's a Foundation

Unlike the sword of the Spirit, which actively cuts, the belt of truth is passive in appearance—but critical in function. It does not need to swing. It needs only to hold. And when it holds, the rest of the armor stays in place.

Without truth, righteousness becomes self-righteousness.

Without truth, peace becomes tolerance.

Without truth, faith becomes superstition.

Without truth, salvation becomes sentiment.

Without truth, the sword becomes abusive.

Without truth, prayer becomes manipulation.

So before we speak, we must stand. Before we defend, we must discern. Before we run, we must be rooted.

The Loins: Symbol of Reproduction and Strength

In Hebrew thought, the loins were often seen as the place of generational power. To be girded in the loins is to be prepared for continuity and fruitfulness. The belt of truth is not simply for battle—it is for birthing. It is what allows the next generation to inherit not confusion, but clarity.

Truth is reproductive. Lies are destructive. When truth girds us, what we birth—our words, works, legacy—is aligned with heaven. And when we abandon truth, we birth Ishmaels—solutions that seem wise but are not blessed.

This is why truth must tighten us—not loosely wrapped, but fastened with commitment.

In a World of Relativism

We live in a world that says "your truth" and "my truth." But the belt does not flex for opinion. The belt does not widen for culture. It fits only the measurements of God's unchanging Word.

To wear the belt of truth is to offend falsehood. It is to be willing to be called rigid, outdated, or extreme. But we do not fasten our belts to gain applause. We fasten them because eternity demands it.

In a courtroom of shifting narratives, the belt of truth remains the only thing that keeps the spiritual garments from falling.

Christ, the Truth

Jesus did not say, "I know the truth." He said, "I am the truth."
—John 14:6

To put on the belt of truth is to wrap yourself in Christ. To refuse the belt is to reject the One who embodies it. Truth is not a concept. Truth is a Person. And He is not adjustable.

The prophets wore it. The apostles died for it. The saints of history were martyred by it. And we, in this generation, must not treat it as an accessory. It is the first piece for a reason: truth determines all else.

How to Gird Yourself Today

- Begin with confession — Name the lies you've believed. Expose the contradictions you've tolerated.

- Tighten your convictions — Let Scripture set your boundaries. Do not apologize for believing what God has spoken.

- Secure your speech — Let your "yes be yes." Refuse flattery, gossip, and compromise.

- Ask for the Spirit of Truth — The Holy Spirit is not just Comforter but Corrector. Let Him adjust your belt daily.

"Buy the truth, and sell it not; also wisdom, and instruction, and understanding."
—Proverbs 23:23

In a world falling apart at the seams, let us be the ones whose armor never slips—because truth is tight, firm, and fastened.

Let every generation behind us know: we stood.

—DBC

Chapter II
The Breastplate of Righteousness —
Guarding the Heart of the Called

"And having on the breastplate of righteousness..."
—Ephesians 6:14 (KJV)

The Shield Over the Heart

Righteousness is not simply right behavior. It is a divine position. It is not the polish of human effort, but the armor of divine covering. When Paul instructs the believer to wear the "breastplate of righteousness," he is not calling for moral perfection, but for protection grounded in justification.

The breastplate guards the heart. And the heart, according to Scripture, is the wellspring of life. "Keep thy heart with all diligence," writes Solomon, "for out of it are the issues of life." (Proverbs 4:23)

What protects the heart is not sentiment, but sanctity. It is righteousness— not opinion, not self-worth, not popularity, but the declared innocence granted by the righteousness of Christ.

In Bloodline, I wrote of the incorruptible blood that secured our redemption. Righteousness is the robe purchased by that blood. In The Remnant, I described how the holy ones are marked—not by outward religiosity but by inward consecration. The breastplate is not made of human metal. It is forged by grace.

Not Our Righteousness

Isaiah is clear:

> *"All our righteousnesses are as filthy rags."*
> *—Isaiah 64:6*

The Apostle Paul reiterates this when he says:

> *"Not having mine own righteousness...but that which is*
> *through the faith of Christ."*
> *—Philippians 3:9*

To wear the breastplate is to reject self-righteousness and receive Christ's righteousness.

This armor is not earned—it is given. But to keep it shining, we must walk in the Spirit. Though imputed righteousness covers us legally, imparted righteousness transforms us spiritually.

Legal standing and spiritual condition—both are needed. One protects. The other empowers.

What Does It Mean to Be Righteous?

- It means to agree with God's definition of right and wrong.

- It means to live in alignment with His nature.

- It means to reject the applause of man for the approval of God.

- It means to guard your inner life so your outer witness remains untainted.

The breastplate is not flexible. It is not fashionable. It is not trend-sensitive. It is firm, weighty, and radiant.

In a world that says, "Follow your heart," righteousness replies, "Protect it first."

The Heart as the Battlefield

Satan does not always aim for your sword hand—he aims for your chest. He aims for your affections, your convictions, your emotions, your loyalties. If your heart is compromised, the whole body falters.

That is why the breastplate is critical. It covers the vital organ of your soul. It absorbs the arrow. It deflects the insult. It shields the wound.

In The Voice in the Wilderness, I spoke of Elijah's moment of collapse— not because he lost his calling, but because his heart was overwhelmed. Had his heart not been guarded by righteousness, he would have perished. Instead, he found God not in the fire, but in the whisper—because righteousness anchors the heart to God, not to the storm.

Holiness as the Material

Though the breastplate is positional righteousness, it is woven in the thread of holiness. Holiness is not a denomination—it is the very nature of God infused into the life of the believer.

In God's Sovereignty, I wrote that the throne of God is built on justice and righteousness. He does not call His people to be clever or powerful first—but to be holy as He is holy.

Thus, the armor reflects its source: it glows with the purity of the One who gave it.

What Happens When You Remove the Breastplate?

- The heart grows hard, or worse, cold.

- Sin begins to feel normal.

- The voice of the Spirit fades.

- Identity fractures.

- Conviction weakens.

To remove righteousness is to invite death at the level of the soul.

When David repented after his fall with Bathsheba, he cried, "Create in me a clean heart, O God." (Psalm 51:10) He did not ask for his crown back. He asked for his righteousness back. He knew the breastplate had been removed—and he wanted it restored.

Righteousness as Light in the Darkness

To wear the breastplate of righteousness is to walk in clarity in a world of confusion. It is to shine even when the culture darkens. It is to guard your heart—not with cynicism, but with consecration.

And when the enemy comes with accusations, righteousness silences him.

> *"Who shall lay any thing to the charge of God's elect? It is God that justifieth."*
> *—Romans 8:33*

When Satan accuses you of your past, lift your chin and point to your armor. It was not made in your strength. It was forged at Calvary. And it does not rust.

How to Keep the Breastplate Bright

- Repent quickly — Don't let sin linger. Confession cleanses the armor.

- Practice holiness — Let your heart remain tender to His voice.

- Reject self-righteousness — Clothe yourself in Christ, not performance.

- Receive the righteousness daily — It's not a one-time suit; it's a daily garment.

> *"Put ye on the Lord Jesus Christ..."*
> *—Romans 13:14*

To wear the breastplate is to say: My heart is not for sale. My heart is sealed. My heart is guarded by righteousness.

This is not just protection—it is identity.

It tells every power of darkness: This one is covered.

Chapter III
The Shoes of the Gospel of Peace — Prepared for Movement

"And your feet shod with the preparation of the gospel of peace."
—Ephesians 6:15 (KJV)

The Feet of Readiness

The armor of God includes not only defense but propulsion. The shoes Paul describes are not ornamental sandals—they are designed for movement, terrain, and impact. These are shoes of readiness, forged in the peace of the gospel and strapped with the intent to go forward.

Peace is not passive. It is a force that advances the kingdom. It is not the absence of noise, but the presence of divine order. These gospel shoes do not only carry good news—they embody a life prepared to walk in it.

In Yeshua the Builder, we traced the Messiah's early years—how He walked through dust and rejection, yet carried peace as purpose. And in The Bread of Life, we followed Him to Bethlehem and back—never stationary, always moving with divine intent. That same motion now transfers to the believer.

Preparedness Is Power

The word preparation (Greek: ἑτοιμασία, hetoimasia) means foundation, readiness, or firm footing. These shoes are not decorative—they anchor the soldier in rough terrain. Roman soldiers nailed studs or cleats into their soles for traction. Why?

Because slippery feet lose battles.

Likewise, spiritual warfare requires grip—the ability to stand, pivot, and press forward when the ground shifts. The gospel of peace provides this grounding.

Peace is not weakness. It is the strategy of heaven against the chaos of hell.

Peace Is a Weapon

In Selective Outrage, we exposed the culture's addiction to anger. In contrast, peace disarms rage. The enemy thrives on noise, confusion, and panic. But peace—true gospel peace—is the shockwave of calm in the center of spiritual battle.

Paul said in Romans 16:20:

> *"And the God of peace shall bruise Satan under your feet shortly."*

Notice that? It is not the God of war who crushes the serpent—it is the God of peace. Peace, rooted in truth, is lethal to deception.

When you walk in peace, you walk with unshakable authority.

The Gospel as Footwear

The shoes are made of gospel. That means:

- You walk in forgiveness, not shame.
- You walk in authority, not fear.
- You walk carrying good news, not confusion.
- You walk with purpose, not wanderlust.

Isaiah 52:7 proclaims:

> *"How beautiful upon the mountains are the feet of him that bringeth good tidings, that publisheth peace..."*

Peace is not just what you have—it's what you carry.

The Peace of Christ, the Path of Purpose

Yeshua's life was marked by steps—each one preordained. He walked from Nazareth to Jordan, from wilderness to Galilee, from garden to Golgotha. And all the while, His feet carried peace, even in pain.

When the winds rose on Galilee, He walked on the waves. Why? Because peace walks above the chaos.

In The Bread of Life, we saw how He walked toward the broken. Not away from them. These are the shoes you now wear. You are not just called to survive spiritual battle—you are called to advance through it.

Peace is how we take ground.

The Terrain of the Gospel

Peace doesn't mean the terrain is soft. On the contrary, the gospel sends us into:

- Wildernesses — places of testing
- Mountains — places of encounter
- Valleys — places of deep trust
- Cities — places of witness

Your shoes must be tough enough for every terrain. The gospel is not seasonal—it is eternal footwear. Wherever you walk, you carry the message of reconciliation.

> *"And, having made peace through the blood of his*
> *cross..."*
> *—Colossians 1:20*

Your feet are now dipped in blood-bought peace. You are a mobile ambassador of heaven's kingdom.

Peace in Preparation, Not Perfection

Preparation does not mean perfection—it means intentional posture. Soldiers do not wait for battles to break out to lace their boots. They sleep with them ready.

Likewise, peace is not something you put on when the storm hits. It's something you wear before the trumpet sounds.

In The Mountain Still Speaks, we learned that those who listen to the Word and obey it are like wise men who build their house on the rock. The same is true for our footing. Peace must be our ground—not after the rain, but before it falls.

When Peace Walks into the Room

There is a peculiar authority on a believer who walks in peace:

- They deescalate chaos.

- They discern truth in the fog.

- They remain calm under fire.

- They become the environment, not the victim of it.

This is not natural personality—it is supernatural fruit.
"The fruit of the Spirit is... peace."
—Galatians 5:22

The March of the Saints

The early Church moved forward in peace, even under persecution. Paul and Silas sang in jail. Stephen prayed for his killers. The disciples walked in joy after being beaten.

Why? Because their feet were shod with something otherworldly.

In every book I've written, from Divine Encounters to The Mystery of Mysteries, I have emphasized this singular truth:

Peace is the rhythm of the throne room.

Those who walk with God do not rush. They stride. They march. They tread on serpents with confidence. Their steps release the aroma of heaven.

Final Charge: Step With Intention

- Do not stumble—let peace correct your gait.

- Do not wander—let peace guide your direction.

- Do not hesitate—let peace hasten your obedience.

> *"Great peace have they which love thy law: and nothing*
> *shall offend them."*
> *—Psalm 119:165*

With peace underfoot, nothing can shake you. The gospel is your footing. The cross is your compass. And your steps—no matter how weary—leave eternal prints.

—DBC

Chapter IV
The Shield of Faith —
The Extinguisher of Fiery Lies

*"Above all, taking the shield of faith, wherewith ye shall
be able to quench all the fiery darts of the wicked."*
—Ephesians 6:16 (KJV)

Faith Is Not Fragile

The apostle Paul says, "Above all"—not as a matter of hierarchy, but of
urgency. When the enemy fires his darts—those deceptive, flaming
accusations and attacks—faith is not merely helpful. It is essential.

This shield is not a decorative emblem. It is a full-body defense forged in
belief and trust. Without faith, you are exposed. With faith, you are
covered.

In Three Weapons and a Stone, I wrote about how David's trust in the
Name of the Lord was stronger than Goliath's sword. In Chapter 2: The
Weapons of the Spirit, the stone was glowing not with force, but with
faith. This shield Paul describes is that same trust—made visible.

The Nature of the Shield

In Roman warfare, soldiers used a scutum—a large, curved shield that
covered the body from chin to shin. They soaked it in water before battle,
so that incoming fire-tipped arrows would be extinguished on impact.

This is the image Paul draws on. The believer is not to fight unprotected. Your faith must be:

- Soaked in the Word
- Held in both hands
- Moved with precision
- Used in formation

You don't wave your faith like a magic wand—you stand behind it like a fortress.

Fiery Darts Defined

What are these darts?

- Lies about your identity
- Accusations from the past
- Doubts about God's goodness
- Fear of man or failure
- Temptations that distract or seduce
- Disappointments that lead to disillusionment

The enemy's darts come flaming and fast. But they only burn what is unshielded.

This is why faith must go before you.

> *"For we walk by faith, not by sight."*
> *—2 Corinthians 5:7*

Faith sees the unseen. It absorbs the blow. It answers the devil's shout with God's whisper.

When Faith Fails, Fire Spreads

In Selective Outrage, I explained how selective belief produces selective justice. The same is true in the spirit: when faith is partial, fire invades. Doubt spreads like a contagion. Fear multiplies where belief collapses.

That's why Paul says, Above all… You cannot afford to be passive with your faith. It must be trained. Maintained. Raised.

Faith Is Not Just a Belief — It Is a Barrier

Faith is not a warm feeling or positive thinking. It is a strategic defense.

It says:

- "I believe what God said more than what I feel."

- "I believe in His promise more than in my pain."

- "I believe in His Word more than the world's headlines."

In The Voice in the Wilderness, I showed how prophets shielded their generations by standing behind the promises of God. Elijah prayed for fire not because he was dramatic—but because his faith made room for God to act.

So too, your faith is the shield that makes heaven's power operational.

Faith Must Be Lifted

Notice Paul says: "Taking the shield…" That means it must be:

- Consciously grabbed

- Daily raised

- Proactively wielded

It is possible to have a shield and not use it. Too many believers are pierced not because they lack faith, but because they've left it on the ground.

You must take it up.

Corporate Faith, Unbreakable Wall

In Roman phalanx formation, soldiers interlocked their shields to create a mobile fortress. The Church is meant to do the same.

Your shield is stronger when it joins with others. When you stand side-by-side with brothers and sisters in the faith, you create an unbreakable wall.

In Mountain Still Speaks, we saw that private faith builds public strength. Your personal trust is not just for you—it empowers the body.

> *"Let us hold fast the profession of our faith without*
> *wavering... and let us consider one another to*
> *provoke unto love and to good works."*
> *—Hebrews 10:23-24*

Faith in Action: Three Examples

1. Noah built the ark when there was no rain.

His shield of faith absorbed the ridicule of generations.

2. Abraham believed for a son though his body was dead.

His shield extinguished every dart of biological doubt.

3. The woman with the issue of blood pressed through the crowd. Her faith overcame social shame, illness, and fear.

These are shields in motion. Not just protection—but momentum.

The Victory Is in the Quenching

Paul promises not only that we'll be hit, but that we'll overcome the hit.

> *"You shall be able to quench all the fiery darts..."*

Not some. All.

Faith doesn't prevent attacks. It renders them powerless.

In The Mystery of Mysteries, I explored how the unseen shapes the visible. The shield of faith is the unseen barrier that changes the trajectory of every visible arrow.

Final Charge: Raise It Today

- Faith is forged in the fire of obedience.

- It is stretched through trials.

- It is empowered by truth.

- And it becomes visible when tested.

"Now faith is the substance of things hoped for, the
evidence of things not seen."
—Hebrews 11:1

Your shield is not ornamental. It is elemental. The moment you raise it, heaven leans in. Hell backs off.

Hold it firm. Soak it in Scripture. Quench every dart. And never fight without it.

—DBC

Chapter V
The Helmet of Salvation —
Mind Secured by Eternity

"And take the helmet of salvation..."
—Ephesians 6:17 (KJV)

The War of the Mind

If Satan cannot destroy you, he will attempt to confuse you. His strategy is ancient: distort truth, inject fear, plant lies, and disorient the mind.

The helmet of salvation is not merely about going to heaven. It is about having your thoughts governed by eternal truth, now.

Paul knew that believers needed more than defense against external weapons. They needed divine protection from internal war—the battle for the mind.

This helmet guards your thought life, your identity, and your destiny.

What Is Salvation?

Salvation is not only the forgiveness of sin; it is the total rescue and restoration of the human being by the blood of Yeshua. It includes:

- Justification (past)
- Sanctification (present)
- Glorification (future)

The helmet reminds you: You are saved.

The enemy wants you to forget that. He wants your thoughts tied to shame, not grace. To trauma, not transformation.

The helmet tells you: You belong to God.

You are covered. You are delivered. You are sealed.

The Battle for Clarity

In The Mystery of Mysteries, I examined how divine design begins at the head. The skull, like the temple, is sacred space. The brain is not just biology—it is the seat of command.

Without the helmet, every dart of the enemy lands in your mind:

- "You're not really saved."

- "God won't use you."

- "You're too far gone."

- "You'll always be broken."

But salvation is a crown, not a question mark. When worn properly, it blocks doubt and crowns you with truth.

> *"Thou, O Lord, art a shield for me; my glory, and the lifter up of mine head."*
> *—Psalm 3:3*

Christ—The Mind of Salvation

Paul wrote to the Philippians:

> *"Let this mind be in you, which was also in Christ Jesus..."*
> *—Philippians 2:5*

Yeshua wore a "helmet" of divine purpose. Even when mocked with a crown of thorns, He did not waver in His identity. That's salvation thinking.

To wear the helmet is to adopt His mind:

- Humble but royal

- Obedient but strong

- Broken yet undefeated

Renewing the Mind Is Warfare

Romans 12:2 says:

> *"Be ye transformed by the renewing of your mind..."*

The enemy wants to poison the mind. God wants to renew it.

- In Son of Man, we learned Christ came not just to save bodies but to restore minds.

- In The Bread of Life, His Word fed minds hungry for more than law.

- In Divine Encounters, every name of God reveals truth that renews and protects thought patterns.

The helmet of salvation is a mindset of deliverance. Every time you put it on, you declare:

> *"I am no longer a slave to fear. My mind belongs to the Lord."*

Mental Attacks Are Real

We often neglect that spiritual warfare manifests as:

- Anxiety

- Insecurity

- Mental fatigue

- Confusion about calling

- Persistent hopelessness

But Paul writes in 1 Thessalonians 5:8:

> *"For a helmet, the hope of salvation."*

Hope is not fantasy—it is the protective lining of your mind.

The Helmet and Identity

In Bloodline, I explored how identity in Christ is tied to spiritual lineage. The helmet of salvation secures that identity. When you wear it, you stop asking:

- "Am I good enough?"
- "Do I belong?"
- "Is God still with me?"

You begin declaring:

- "I am a new creation."
- "I am redeemed."
- "I have the mind of Christ."

The helmet changes inner monologue into divine decree.

It Must Be Taken

Paul writes: "Take the helmet…"

That means you must:

1. Acknowledge you need it
2. Pick it up daily
3. Place it over every thought
4. Refuse to take it off

You don't wear the helmet just on Sundays. You wear it when you face fear. When you're tired. When lies whisper. When doubt screams.

Put it on again.

Helmet as Final Guard

When all else fails—when shield shakes, sword slips, or knees wobble—the helmet is often the last line of defense. In Roman battle, a well-forged helmet could be the only thing between life and death in a final blow.

So too with salvation. It holds when nothing else does.

"He hath covered me with the helmet of salvation."
—Isaiah 59:17

Declare It Daily

Let this be your proclamation:

I wear salvation like a crown.

My thoughts are guarded.

My identity is sealed.

My mind is not for rent to lies.

I think with the mind of Christ.

I walk with the hope of eternity.

I live by the finished work of the Cross.

This helmet is mine. And I will not take it off.

—DBC

Chapter VI
The Sword of the Spirit —
The Spoken Word That Cuts

"...and the sword of the Spirit, which is the word of God."
—Ephesians 6:17 (KJV)

No Soldier Fights Without a Sword

Armor is for defense. But the sword? That's for dominion.

Paul, chained to Roman guards, understood this one truth: you can be protected, covered, sealed, and prepared—but if you do not speak, you cannot strike.

The sword of the Spirit is not a human weapon. It is divine speech—living, breathing, unshakable Word. And it is the only offensive piece in the list.

Everything else keeps the enemy out.

The sword drives him back.

Logos and Rhema: Two Edges of the Blade

In The Words of Jesus and Divine Encounters, I explored the two biblical words for "word":

- Logos – the eternal, unchanging Word of God

- Rhema – the spoken, timely, Spirit-breathed utterance

The sword you hold is both:

1. Logos is the full sword: forged in eternity, it never breaks.

2. Rhema is the swing: used in battle, it pierces the lie now.

> *"For the word of God is quick, and powerful, and sharper*
> *than any twoedged sword..."*
> *—Hebrews 4:12*

This Sword Cuts Both Ways

The Word cuts through:

- Lies and truth

- Darkness and light

- Deception and clarity

- Flesh and spirit

- Soul and bone

But it also pierces you first. Before it changes the world, it carves the heart.

To carry the sword of the Spirit is to let God's Word convict you, cleanse you, and commission you.

Christ—The Word Made Flesh

In the Gospels, we do not merely see Christ carrying a sword. He is the sword.

> *"Out of his mouth went a sharp twoedged sword..."*
> *—Revelation 1:16*

He speaks, and storms stop.

He speaks, and demons flee.

He speaks, and dead men rise.

He speaks, and the world shifts.

The sword is not merely the book—it is the breath behind the book.

It is the voice of God, alive in His people.

You Must Speak

The enemy fears silence less than Spirit-saturated speech.

In Three Weapons and a Stone, we saw this principle in action. David did not only throw a stone—he declared a name:

> *"Thou comest to me with a sword... but I come to thee in the name of the Lord of hosts..."*
> *—1 Samuel 17:45*

The sword of the Spirit is not physical—it is verbal.

No believer can fight in silence.

Declare the Word. Shout the truth. Swing the sword.

When Jesus Was Tempted

Satan approached Yeshua with Scripture—but twisted.

Jesus responded with:

"It is written…"

"It is written…"

"It is written…"

Three strikes.

Three swings of the sword.

And the devil fled.

He did not argue.

He did not philosophize.

He spoke Rhema from Logos—the right Word at the right time.

> *"Man shall not live by bread alone, but by every word that proceedeth out of the mouth of God."*
> *—Matthew 4:4*

The Sword Is for the Spirit-Filled

You cannot wield this weapon in the flesh.

The sword of the Spirit belongs to the Spirit-led.

- Not just memorized, but internalized

- Not just quoted, but lived

- Not just read, but revealed

In Divine Encounters, I traced how God revealed His names not through silence, but through spoken revelation. Each name is a strike. Each declaration, a weapon.

Why Many Believers Feel Powerless

Because their Bible stays closed.

Their mouth stays shut.

Their mind stays unrenewed.

To reclaim your sword:

1. Know the Word – Logos

2. Hear the Spirit – Rhema

3. Speak with boldness – Faith

4. Live in holiness – Alignment

5. Strike with precision – Wisdom

In the Final Battle

Revelation 19 describes the return of Christ:

> *"...and out of his mouth goeth a sharp sword, that with it he should smite the nations..."*

He doesn't need artillery. He speaks—and armies collapse.

This is your weapon, too.

This is the sword that cast Lucifer from heaven.

This is the Word that opened the tomb.

This is the breath that formed the cosmos.

And it is in your mouth, if you believe.

Let the Sword Speak

I wield the sword of the Spirit.

My Bible is not decoration.

It is declaration.

I do not fight with fists—I fight with faith.

I do not win by silence—I win by Scripture.

The Word of God is my weapon.

And I will speak it until the darkness flees.

—DBC

Chapter VII
Praying Always in the Spirit — The Invisible Weapon

"Praying always with all prayer and supplication in the Spirit..."
—Ephesians 6:18 (KJV)

Unseen Yet Unmatched

Paul closes the list of armor with something that seems outside the wardrobe—but in truth, it is the thread that binds it all.

Prayer is not merely an action. It is the atmosphere of the battle.

It is the unseen power behind every piece.

The belt is fastened, the breastplate is shining, the shield is lifted—but without prayer, the soldier is unplugged from command.

Prayer is the invisible weapon—and yet, in the spirit realm, it shakes foundations.

Not Just Prayer—But in the Spirit

There are many who pray, but few who know how to pray in the Spirit:

- Not routine recitation, but revelation-born intercession

- Not emotional panic, but spiritual perception

- Not self-centered murmurs, but God-centered warfare

In The Mountain Still Speaks, especially in the chapters on "When You Pray" and "Enter Into Thy Closet," I revealed the difference between vain repetition and sacred communion.

To pray in the Spirit is to enter the battle from heaven's vantage point.

Heaven's Communication Line

Prayer is not about informing God. It is about aligning with Him.

When you pray in the Spirit, you:

- Tune into heaven's frequency

- Discern hidden strategies

- Intercept enemy plans

- Activate divine intervention

Jesus often withdrew to pray—not because He lacked power, but because power flows from communion.

> *"But Jesus often withdrew to lonely places and prayed."*
> *—Luke 5:16*

In solitude, He received strength.

In silence, He heard strategy.

In surrender, He gained supremacy.

David and the Secret Weapon

In Three Weapons and a Stone, we never saw David stop to pray during the visible battle—but we know, by his confidence and clarity, that he had already prayed.

Before he ran to Goliath, he had run to God.

> *"I sought the LORD, and he heard me, and delivered me*
> *from all my fears."*
> *—Psalm 34:4*

His victory in public was rooted in secret communion.

How to Pray in the Spirit

1. Surrender your mind – let the Spirit guide your thoughts

2. Saturate in the Word – let Scripture shape your prayers

3. Listen more than you speak – revelation flows from silence

4. Speak what He gives – prophecy, intercession, tongues

5. Stay in posture – warfare is not momentary; it's constant

In Divine Encounters, I chronicled how many of God's breakthroughs came when people stayed in prayer: Hannah, Elijah, Daniel, Jesus in Gethsemane.

Why the Enemy Fears This Most

Satan fears your sword. But he trembles at your connection.

Because the one who prays:

- Hears divine strategy

- Shuts down deception

- Births revivals

- Sees chains break

- Brings heaven to earth

Paul does not separate prayer from armor—he concludes the armor with it.

The soldier of God is not complete until they are communing with the Commander.

Prayer Is Not Optional for Warriors

It is not a break between battles.

It is the battle itself.

To walk in the Spirit is to pray in the Spirit.

To be filled with the Spirit is to war in prayer.

The early Church did not organize programs—they devoted themselves to prayer and the Word (Acts 6:4).

A Soldier on His Knees

The most dangerous figure in the Kingdom is not the loudest preacher or the most visible prophet. It is the hidden intercessor, the unseen warrior who cries out in the night.

- They birth victories no one sees
- They guard cities with groanings
- They hold back hell with hallelujahs

When you pray in the Spirit, you are not escaping reality—you are reshaping it.

The Invisible Weapon in You

Paul said "praying always."

That means in the morning, at work, in sorrow, on the mountain, in the valley.

"Pray without ceasing."
—1 Thessalonians 5:17

This is not burden—it is breath.

It is not drudgery—it is dominion.

You were never meant to fight from earth toward heaven.

You fight from heaven into earth—when you pray in the Spirit.

Prayer Is Victory

I am armed in truth.

I am covered in righteousness.

I walk in peace.

I hold the shield of faith.

I wear the helmet of salvation.

I swing the sword of the Word.

But I breathe in prayer.

Victory begins on my knees.

Power flows from my surrender.

And I will never stop praying in the Spirit.

—DBC

CONCLUSION

Fully Clothed for Glory: The Warrior, the Call, and the Age to Come

There is a moment in every true believer's life when the weight of eternity collides with the urgency of the present. When the call is no longer a whisper behind the veil but a trumpet in the soul. In that moment, the armor of God becomes more than metaphor—it becomes mantle, identity, inheritance, and shield. The call to be fully clothed in divine armor is not poetic—it is prophetic.

The Apostle Paul, writing from the shadows of a Roman prison, did not suggest that believers wear the armor; he commanded it:

> *"Put on the whole armor of God, that ye may be able to*
> *stand against the wiles of the devil."*
> *—Ephesians 6:11*

Paul had seen the church rise. He had seen it stumble. He had seen the warfare, and he knew it was not flesh and blood that stood against them—but powers, principalities, and rulers of the darkness of this age. He knew that every Roman breastplate, every imperial sword, every iron helmet—were fleeting shadows of something infinitely stronger.

The true warrior wears unseen glory.

The eternal soldier moves not by strength of hand but by fire of the Spirit and truth.

The armor of God is not forged by men—it is breathed from Heaven.

The Warrior

You, believer, are not a bystander in this age. You are not merely "a Christian"—you are a called one, chosen for a war that predates time. From the moment the serpent hissed in Eden and the promise of a bruised head and a crushed heel was spoken, you were written into the cosmic battle. The armor you wear is not given lightly. It is the armor of a Son of the King, a warrior forged in the fire of redemption, not religion.

You are clothed with truth because lies are the currency of this fallen world.

You wear righteousness because compromise cannot shield a tender heart.

You walk in peace because chaos has no hold on the one whose feet walk with purpose.

You raise faith because every fiery dart from hell fears its light.

You wear salvation because your mind belongs not to your past, but to the One who bought you.

And in your hand is the Word—a sword that has split seas, silenced demons, and still pierces hearts.

But more than that— you pray. You breathe Heaven's breath on Earth. You war in the unseen.

And when you stand, clothed in glory… the enemy trembles.

> *"Ye are of God, little children, and have overcome them:*
> *because greater is He that is in you, than he that is in*
> *the world."*
> *—1 John 4:4*

The Call

This armor is not casual wear. It is given for purpose. Paul's imagery was urgent, precise, and costly. Armor is for battle—not for display.

There is a call on this generation. The ground shakes with it. The heavens echo it.

A call to discernment in deception, to courage in chaos, to righteousness in rebellion.

To wear this armor is to say:

"I will not bow. I will not retreat. I will not be silenced."

To wear this armor is to stand in Babylon and not burn, to kneel in Gethsemane and not run, to speak in the temple and not flinch.

It is to live like Daniel, pray like Elijah, walk like Yeshua, and fight like David—not with sword and spear, but with stone and Name.

The armor of God is not antiquated—it is now.

It is not optional—it is essential.

It is not religious—it is revelatory.

The call is not for the few. It is for the Remnant. For the Bride who makes herself ready. For the voice in the wilderness, crying, "Prepare the way of the Lord."

The Age to Come

This age is passing.

Empires are crumbling.

Truth is traded for tolerance.

Good is called evil, and evil wears a smiling mask.

But a new age is rising.

An age not built by politicians or philosophers, but by the King of Glory.

"And I saw heaven opened, and behold a white horse;
and He that sat upon him was called Faithful and
True... and His name is called The Word of God."
—Revelation 19:11,13

The age to come will not be ruled by steel and might, but by the scepter of righteousness.

The King will return not in weakness but in fire and justice.

And the saints will be with Him—clothed in fine linen, righteous and radiant, riding not to retreat, but to reign.

This is why we wear the armor now.

Because we reign then.

We fight now because we will rule with Him.

We suffer now because we will be glorified with Him.

We groan now because the earth is preparing for His arrival.

The armor of God is not just protection.

It is preparation for the coronation.

Final Charge

So, beloved warrior—stand.

Stand when the world mocks.

Stand when your strength is gone.

Stand when your prayers seem silent.

Stand when hell itself throws fire.

And when you've done all… stand still.

Because you are not naked in the storm.

You are not empty in the field.

You are not abandoned in the battle.

You are clothed in the armor of Heaven.

You wear Christ.

You carry the Name.

You move with purpose, you speak with fire, and you belong to eternity.

"But put ye on the Lord Jesus Christ..."
—Romans 13:14

So rise, soldier.

Glory awaits.

And the King is coming

Glossary of Biblical Terms

Abba (אבא)

Aramaic for "Father." A deeply personal term used by Yeshua in the Garden of Gethsemane (Mark 14:36). Denotes intimacy, dependence, and reverence.

See also: The Words of Jesus

Anointing

The divine empowerment or consecration for a task, office, or spiritual purpose. Often marked by oil in the Old Testament and by the Holy Spirit in the New.

Referenced in: I Choose the Call, Yeshua the Builder

Armor of God

The spiritual protection provided to believers as described in Ephesians 6:10–18. Includes truth, righteousness, peace, faith, salvation, the Word, and prayer.

See: Design: The Armor of God

Blood of the Lamb

A reference to Jesus' atoning sacrifice. Spiritually represents cleansing, covenant, and victory.

See also: Bloodline, The Blood That Satan Couldn't Touch

Covenant

A sacred agreement between God and His people, ratified by blood and sealed by divine promise. Includes both Old and New Covenants.

Found in: The Mystery of Mysteries, Divine Encounters

Davidic Line

The royal lineage from David to Yeshua the Messiah. Fulfillment of the promise that a King would reign forever from David's house (2 Samuel 7).

See also: The Bloodline of Redemption

Faith

A conviction of things unseen, the foundation of hope and spiritual action (Hebrews 11:1). The shield of the believer in warfare.

Referenced in: Three Weapons and a Stone, God's Sovereignty

Glory (Hebrew: כָּבוֹד / kabod)

The weight, beauty, and radiant presence of God. Not mere splendor but the essence of His character revealed.

See also: The Mountain Still Speaks, Son of Man

Grace

Unmerited favor and divine empowerment. Not merely leniency but transformative strength to live as God commands.

Discussed in: I Choose the Call, The Lord Is My Shepherd

Gospel

Literally "Good News." The announcement of the Kingdom of God, the reign of Christ, and redemption through His death and resurrection.

Linked to: The Bread of Life, The Words of Jesus

Holiness

The set-apart nature of God and His people. Not merely moral purity, but divine distinction.

Explored in: God's Sovereignty, The Voice in the Wilderness

Jehovah Sabaoth (יְהוָה צְבָאוֹת)

"The LORD of Hosts." A military title for God, Commander of angelic armies. Revealed in times of battle and national crisis.

Central in: Three Weapons and a Stone

Justification

The legal declaration of righteousness through faith in Jesus Christ. A foundational doctrine of salvation.

See also: The Mystery of Mysteries, The Blood Still Speaks

Kingdom of God

The rule and reign of God over all creation, manifest through Christ and His people. Present and future in nature.Discussed in: Yeshua the Builder, The Mountain Still Speaks

Messiah / Mashiach (מָשִׁיחַ)

"Anointed One." The promised Deliverer of Israel and the world. Fulfilled in Jesus of Nazareth.

See: YESHUA: The Nazarene, the Refugee, the Redeemer

New Jerusalem

The redeemed, eternal city described in Revelation 21. Symbol of the Bride, the eternal dwelling of God with man.

Explored in: The Mother of Harlots, Zion Arising (forthcoming)

Righteousness

Right standing before God and the outflow of godly behavior. Both imputed (by Christ) and lived (by the Spirit).

See also: The Lord Is My Shepherd, The Armor of God

Salvation

Deliverance from sin, death, and judgment. A holistic term encompassing past justification, present sanctification, and future glorification.

See: The Bloodline of Redemption, Mystery of Mysteries

Sanctification

The process of becoming holy—set apart unto God. Ongoing work of the Holy Spirit.

Developed in: Divine Encounters, The Voice in the Wilderness

Seed of the Woman

The prophetic promise in Genesis 3:15 foretelling the Messiah who would crush the serpent's head.See also: Bloodline, The Glory Hidden in Flesh

Shekinah

The manifest presence of God, especially in the tabernacle or temple. A post-biblical term rooted in Scripture.

Discussed in: Mystery of Mysteries, The Temple of Man

Shofar

A ram's horn used in worship, warfare, and prophetic declarations. Symbol of awakening and spiritual alertness.

See: Jewish Holidays: Jesus Teaches Us Through Sacred Seasons

Sword of the Spirit

The spoken Word of God, both Logos (written) and Rhema (revealed). A weapon against deception.

Central in: Design: The Armor of God, Words of Jesus

Truth

The eternal standard of God's reality and righteousness. Not subjective but absolute. Embodied in Christ.

See also: Selective Outrage, Let Your Yes Be Yes

Yeshua (יֵשׁוּעַ)

The original Hebrew name of Jesus, meaning "The Lord is Salvation." Emphasizes His Jewish identity and redemptive mission.

See all: YESHUA: The Nazarene, the Refugee, the Redeemer

Also in: The Words of Jesus, The Bread of Life

Scripture Index

(All Scriptures referenced are from the King James Version unless otherwise noted.)

Luke

Luke 4:18 – 108

Luke 10:19 – 170

Luke 22:42 – 147

John

John 1:1 – 113

John 3:16 – 104

John 8:32 – 22, 47

John 14:6 – 23

John 17:17 – 25

Acts

Acts 1:8 – 176

Acts 4:12 – 190

Acts 6:10 – 115

Romans

Romans 1:16 – 132

Romans 5:1 – 134

Romans 6:14 – 128

Romans 8:1 – 126

Romans 10:17 – 99

Romans 12:2 – 69, 130

Romans 13:12 – 41

1 Corinthians

1 Corinthians 1:27 – 118

1 Corinthians 2:4 – 124

1 Thessalonians

2 Timothy

Hebrews

James

1 Peter

Revelation

Visual Appendix

This section contains the official visual plates and symbolic illustrations used throughout the manuscript. Each image is a sacred representation of the spiritual truths expounded in the text, intended for contemplation, clarity, and deeper theological insight. These images reflect the glory of divine design and the majesty of spiritual warfare as revealed in Scripture.

Plate I: The Armor Fully Displayed

A full rendering of the Armor of God as described in Ephesians 6:10–18

- Depicts a warrior in radiant armor standing in the light of dawn.

- Every piece is labeled: Belt of Truth, Breastplate of Righteousness, Shoes of Peace, Shield of Faith, Helmet of Salvation, Sword of the Spirit.

- Inscription at the bottom: "Having done all, to stand." — Ephesians 6:13

- Signature: DBC

Plate II: The Belt of Truth — Girded for Integrity

- A close-up depiction of a radiant belt cinched tightly around the waist, glowing with divine alignment.

- Scriptural connection: "Loins girt about with truth."

- Background: An unshakable path, symbolizing steadfastness.

- Symbolic link: Your writings from Selective Outrage and The Voice in the Wilderness.

Plate III: The Breastplate of Righteousness — Guarding the Heart of the Called

- A shining breastplate with an engraved heart aflame.

- The heart is sealed with a divine emblem representing holiness and purity.

- Background: A battlefield behind, a sanctuary within.

- Connection: Your book Bloodline and chapters on holiness and calling.

Plate IV: The Shoes of the Gospel of Peace — Prepared for Movement

- Sandaled feet firmly planted on a stone path that glows with light.

- Each step leaves a mark of peace.

- Scriptural inscription: "Feet shod with the preparation of the gospel of peace."

- Link to Yeshua the Builder and The Bread of Life.

Plate V: The Shield of Faith — The Extinguisher of Fiery Lies

- A massive shield intercepting arrows of fire mid-air, each arrow labeled with lies like "Fear," "Condemnation," "Doubt."

- The shield glows with an otherworldly strength.

- Caption: "Above all, taking the shield of faith."

- Inspired by Three Weapons and a Stone, especially Chapters 2 & 6.

Plate VI: The Helmet of Salvation — Mind Secured by Eternity

- A glistening helmet encasing the head with celestial stars above.

- Eyes closed, symbolizing peace of mind.

- Etched: "Salvation belongs to the Lord."

- Strong ties to Mystery of Mysteries and Son of Man.

Plate VII: The Sword of the Spirit — The Spoken Word That Cuts

- A gleaming sword mid-swing, with golden script trailing from its edge: "It is written."

- The blade is double-edged, reflecting heaven and earth.

- Captioned: "The Word of God."

- Linked to The Words of Jesus and Divine Encounters.

Plate VIII: The Invisible Weapon — Praying Always in the Spirit

- A warrior kneeling, surrounded by heavenly wind and unseen flames.

- No weapon in hand—only uplifted hands.

- Radiance comes from above, not within.

- Caption: "Praying always with all prayer and supplication in the Spirit."

- Linked to The Mountain Still Speaks and Psalms meditations.

Plate IX: The Warrior Clothed for Glory

- Final unified image: The believer clothed in full armor, standing over the darkness of this age with light bursting from behind the cross.

- Caption: "Fully Clothed for Glory — The Warrior, the Call, and the Age to Come."

- This visual accompanies the book's conclusion and altar call.

NOTE ON PROPORTIONS AND DIAGRAMS

The proportions and diagrams presented in this book are intended to illustrate symbolic, theological, and historical insights drawn from Scripture, art, and sacred geometry. While grounded in anatomical and mathematical research, they represent interpretive models rather than clinical or universally precise measurements of the human body. Their purpose is not to claim absolute scientific accuracy but to reveal the patterns by which artists, architects, and theologians have discerned divine order in creation.

ABOUT THE AUTHOR

Damiano B. Centola is a visionary theologian, poetic thinker, and prophetic voice for this generation. With a rare blend of academic precision and Spirit-filled conviction, his works transcend categories— merging theology, biblical history, art, anatomy, and divine revelation into compelling, world-shifting texts. A prolific author of more than twenty published books, Damiano's writing has been recognized across nations for its bold clarity, prophetic weight, and transformative depth. He has penned landmark works such as The Mystery of Mysteries: Decoding the Divine Proportions of the Human Body, The Bloodline: The Battle for Divine DNA, Selective Outrage, Yeshua the Builder, Jewish Holidays: Jesus Teaches Us Through Sacred Seasons, The Mountain Still Speaks, and Divine Encounters: Discovering the Depth and Power of God's Names. Each project is birthed through deep prayer, years of research, and a fierce commitment to truth.

Damiano is also a speaker, creative strategist, and prophetic author committed to awakening the Church and exposing falsehood with grace and fire. Through his writing and global engagement, he champions the remnant, challenges corruption, and equips believers to walk in truth and power. His heartbeat remains singular: to glorify the name of Jesus Christ, to unveil His majesty in every generation, and to prepare the Bride for the soon-coming King.

He writes from a place of brokenness healed by grace, clarity sharpened by revelation, and a love for the Word that burns unquenchably. Every sentence is meant to point upward—to the Lamb who was slain, who lives, and who reigns.

Damiano B. Centola — DBC

www.ingramcontent.com/pod-product-compliance
Lightning Source LLC
Chambersburg PA
CBHW051235120626
46547CB00013B/1652